Ghost

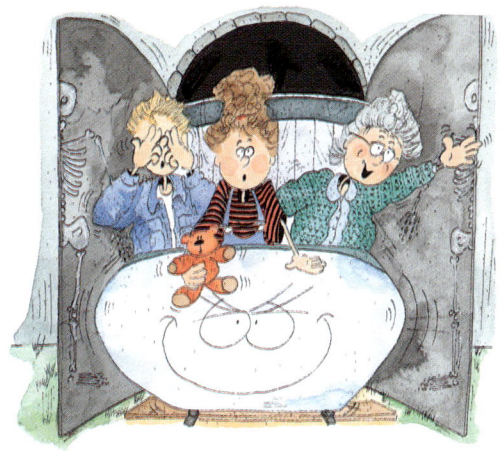

Written by Maire Buonocore

Illustrated by Vanessa Henson

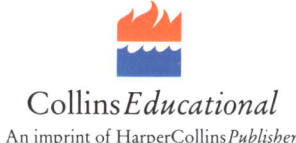

Collins *Educational*

An imprint of HarperCollins *Publishers*

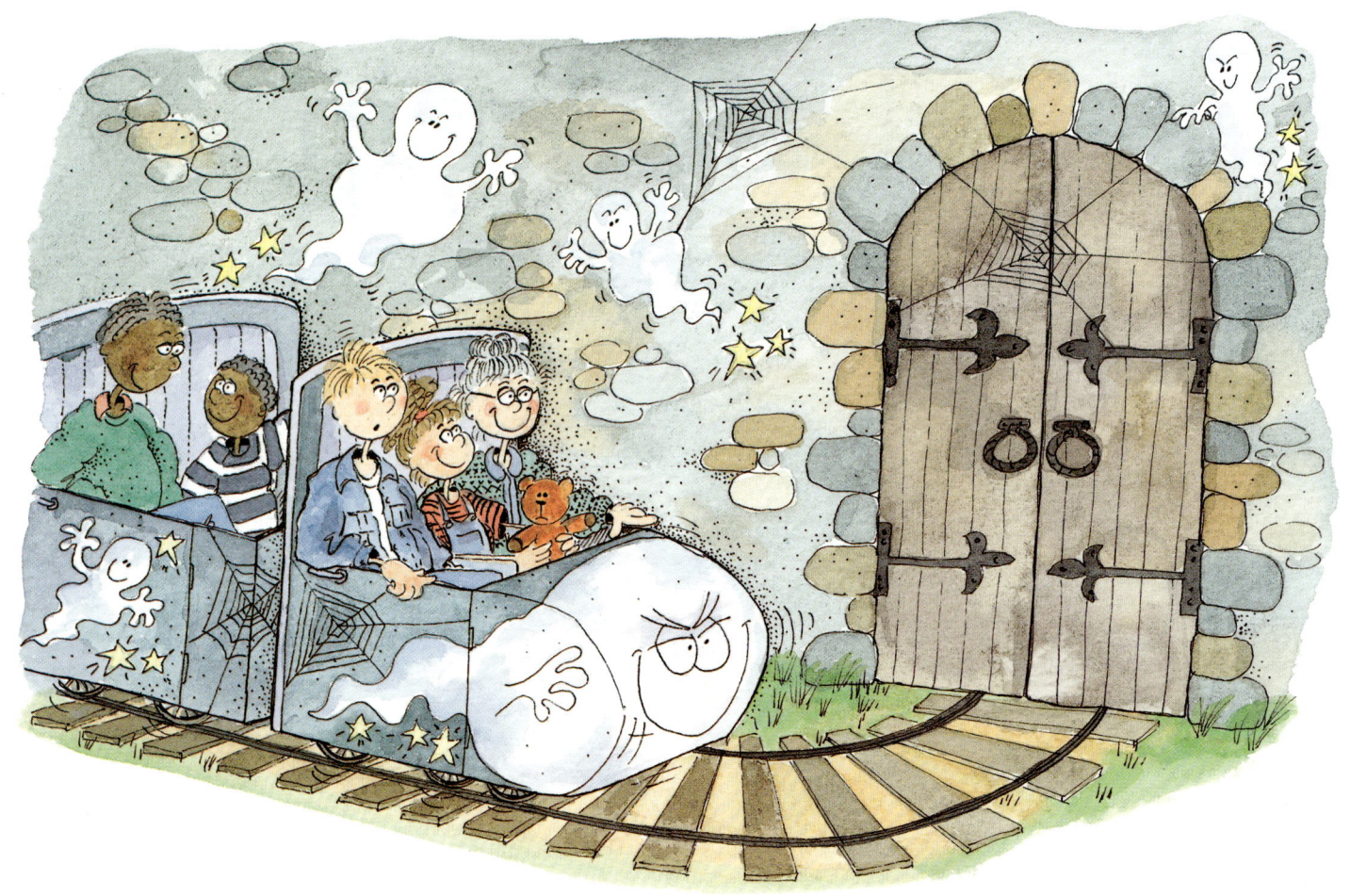

A train.

A door.

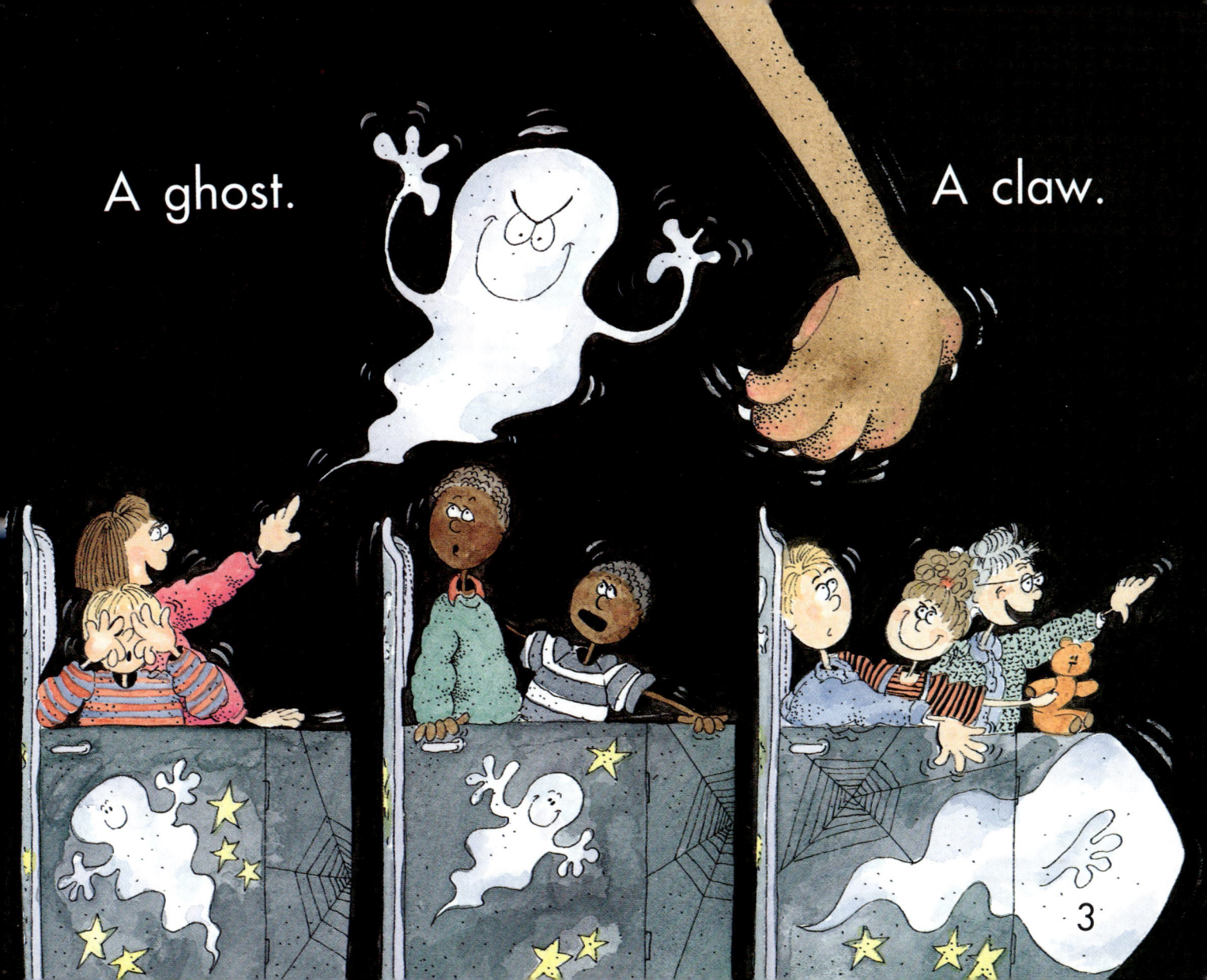

A ghost.

A claw.

3

A web. A bat.

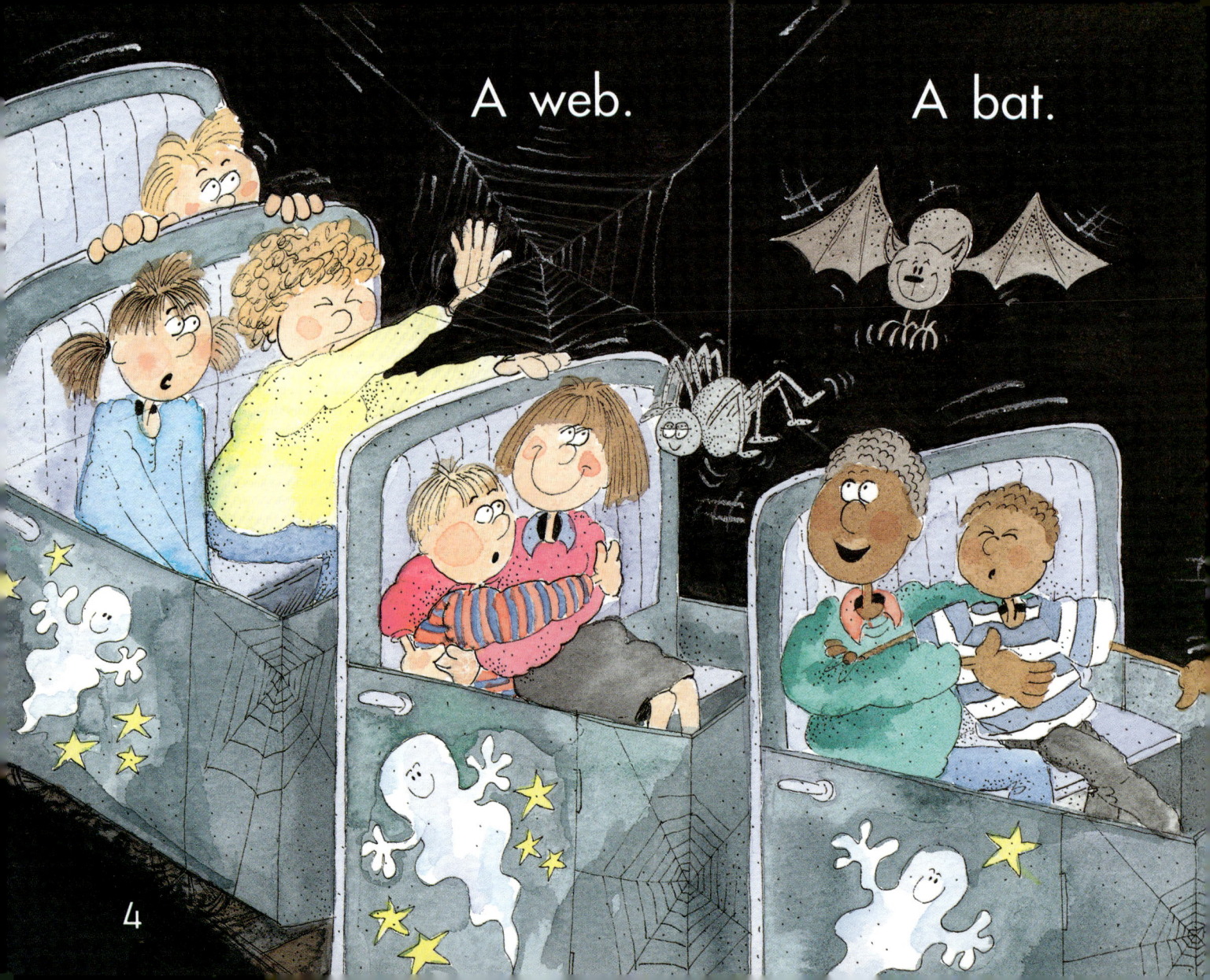

4

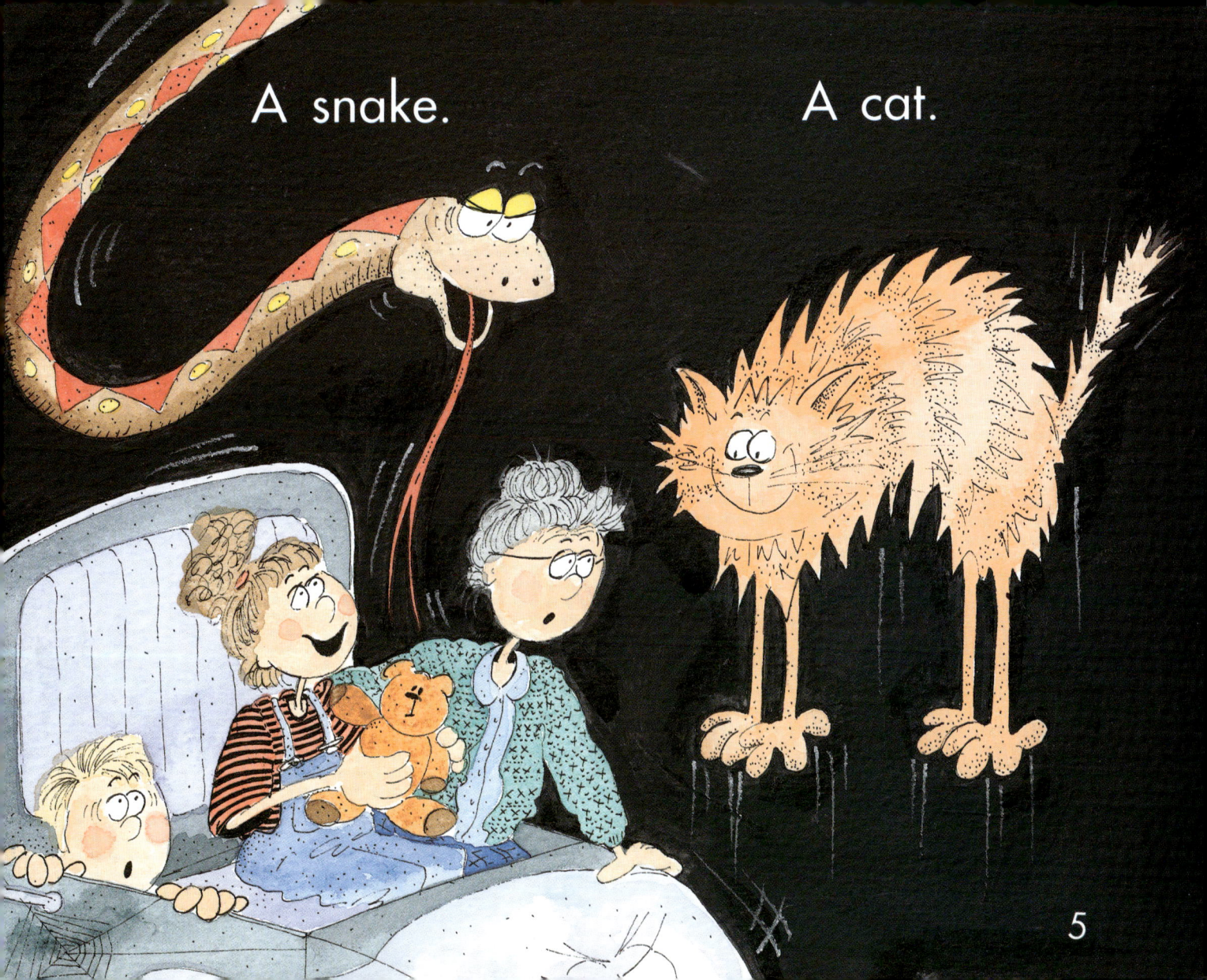

A snake.

A cat.

5

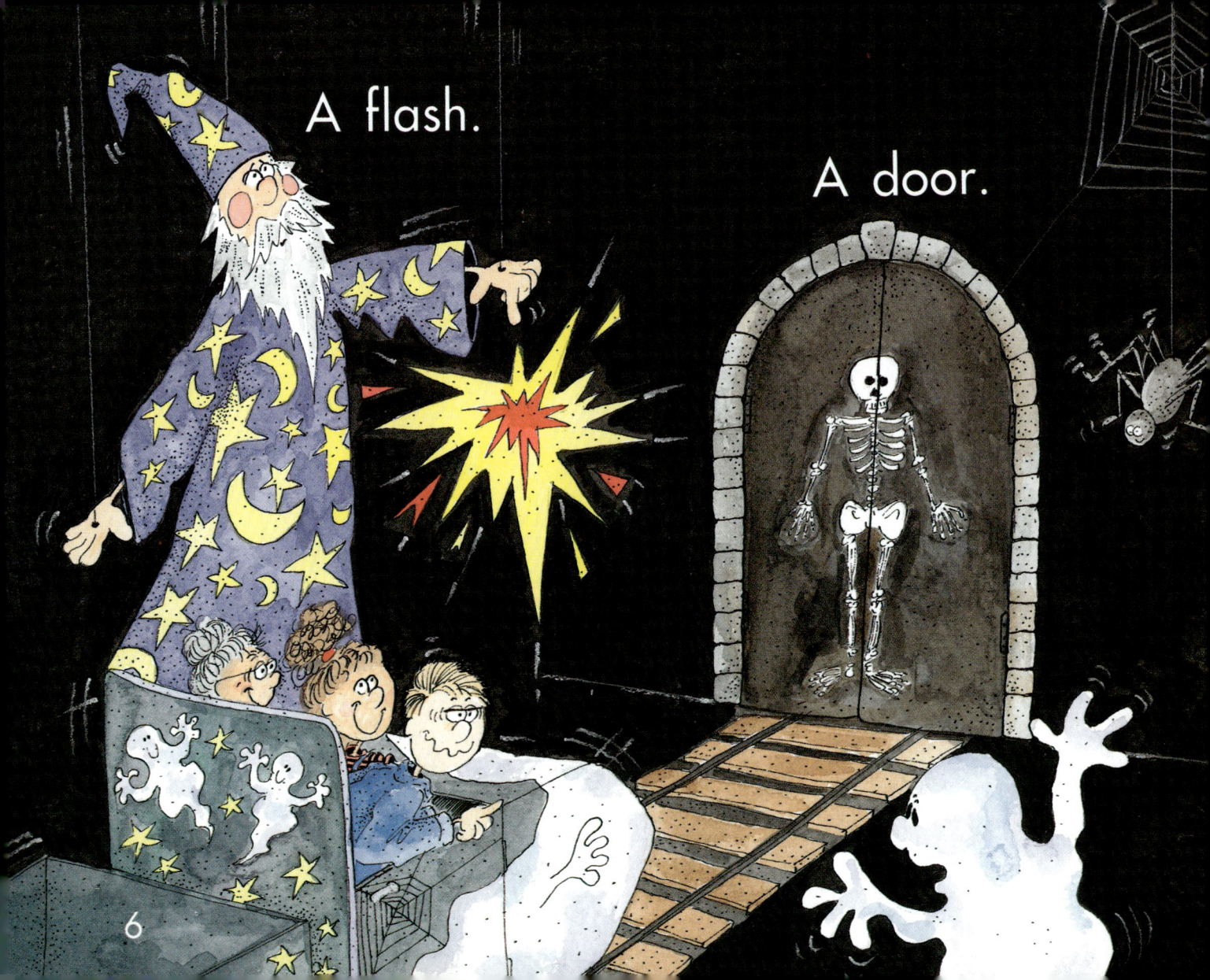

A flash.

A door.

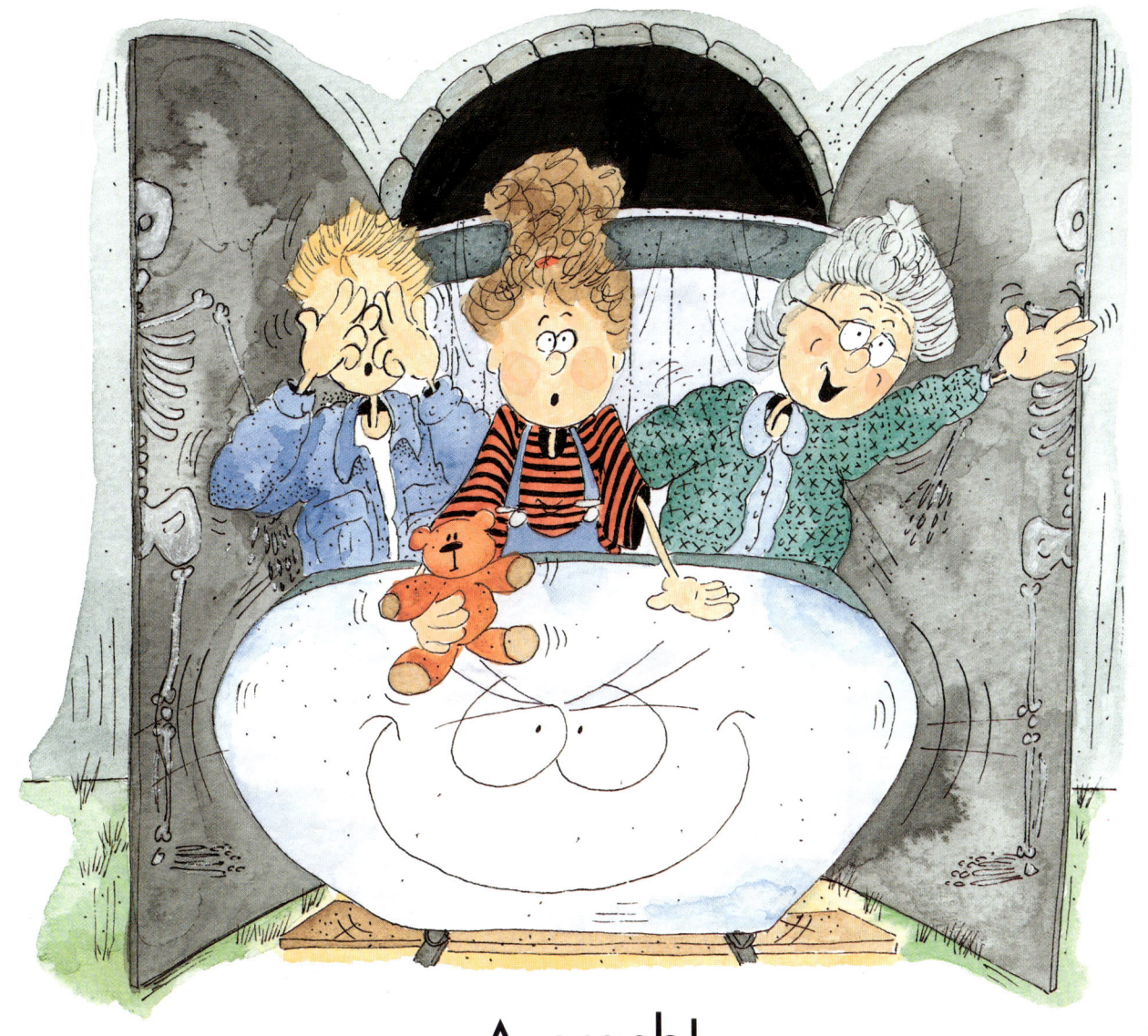

A crash!

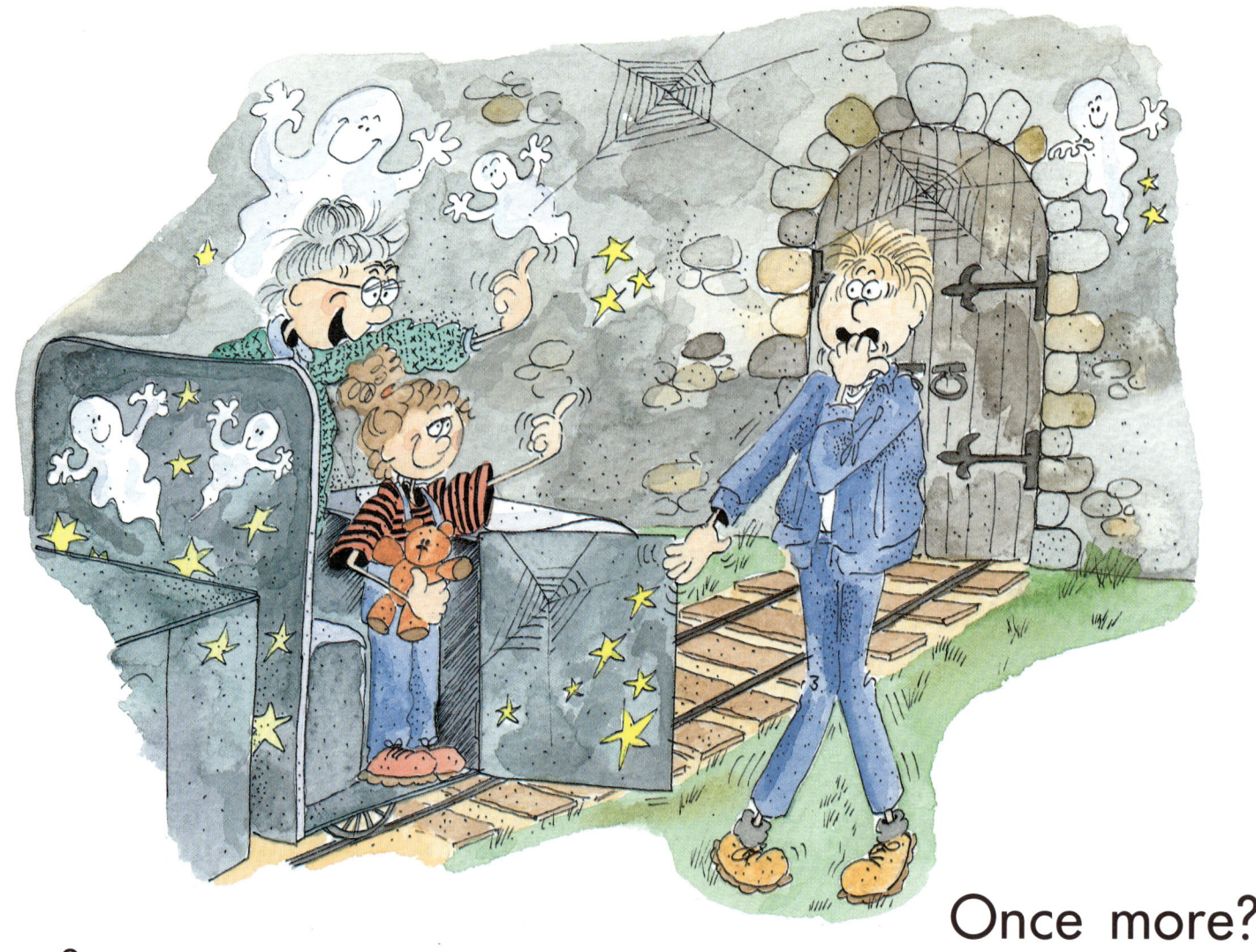

Once more?